Now You Know Science

It's Electric!

Terry Jennings

W
FRANKLIN WATTS
LONDON•SYDNEY

This edition 2013

Franklin Watts
338 Euston Road, London NW1 3BH

Franklin Watts Australia
Level 17/207 Kent St, Sydney, NSW 2000

Copyright © Franklin Watts 2009

Created by Taglines Creative Ltd: Jean Coppendale and Honor Head
Written by: Terry Jennings
Design: Paul Manning

ISBN: 978 1 4451 2319 6

Dewey classification: 537

A CIP catalogue for this book is available from the British Library.

Picture credits
t=top b=bottom l=left r=right

Cover: Indigo Fish, Shutterstock;
3, 14, Monkey Business Images, Shutterstock; 5, 15, Karen Struthers, Shutterstock; 6, Feverpitch, Shutterstock; 7, 28br, Losevsky Pavel, Shutterstock; 8, Yanta, Shutterstock; 9, Losevsky Pavel, Shutterstock; 10, Fedor A. Sidorov, Shutterstock; 11, Alexey Stiop, Shutterstock; 12, 28bl, Rob Byron, Shutterstock; 13, 28tl, Gina Sanders, Shutterstock; 16, 29tr, Martin Muránsky, Shutterstock; 17, 29r, BestWeb, Shutterstock; 18t, Egidijus Skiparis, Shutterstock; 18bl, Pchemyan Georgiy, Shutterstock; 18br, Still Fx, Shutterstock; 19, 28tr, Flashon Studio, Shutterstock; 20, 21, 22, Terry Jennings; 23tl, Monkey Business Images, Shutterstock; 23tr, Jenson, Shutterstock; 23bl, Mariusz Szachowski, Shutterstock; 23br, Ervstock, Shutterstock; 24tl, Marc Dietrich, Shutterstock; 24tr, Mike McDonald, Shutterstock; 24bl, 25, 29tl, Adrian Britton, Shutterstock; 26, Gary 718, Shutterstock; 27, Holger Mette, Shutterstock.

Printed in China

Franklin Watts is a division of Hachette Children's Books, an Hachette UK company.
www.hachette.co.uk

Contents

Electricity at home

We use electricity for many things. Electricity gives us the power to cook our food, heat our water and electric fires, and make our machines work.

▼ **How many things which use electricity can you see in this kitchen?**

We also use electricity to make the lights in our home work.

▲ **An electric light makes the room brighter.**

Heating

Many people switch on an electric fire to keep them warm at home.

hot bars

STOP!
Never touch an electric fire when it is switched on.

▲ When an electric heater is switched on, the bars inside it get red hot.

We also use electricity to heat water to use in the kitchen and the bathroom.

▲ **Electricity heats water in a tank so it runs hot into the bath or shower.**

Food

Food stays fresh for longer inside a fridge.
Electricity keeps the fridge cool.

▲ **Electricity helps us to keep our food fresh inside a fridge.**

Many people use electricity for cooking. This cooker is electric.

STOP!
Keep away from ovens and cooker hobs when they are turned on.

hob

▲ **An electric cooker heats food without any flames or smoke.**

Keeping clean

Electricity makes the machines work that help us to keep our home and clothes clean.

▲ **How would you keep your clothes clean if you didn't have a washing machine?**

We use a vacuum cleaner to keep our floors and carpets clean.

If you had no electricity, how would you keep your floors and carpets clean?

Having fun

Electricity makes our televisions and music systems work.

▲ **Electricity keeps you entertained.**

Without electricity, we would not be able to use our computers or play computer games.

▲ **Everyone can enjoy using a computer because of electricity.**

How it's produced

Most of the electricity we use is produced in a large building called a power station.

▲ **Power stations burn coal, oil or gas to produce electricity.**

Electricity from the power station goes along thick wires. These hang from tall towers called pylons. Thinner wires on wooden poles or under the ground carry the electricity into our homes so that we can use it.

thick wires carry electricity away from the power stations

pylon

Have you seen electricity pylons like these?

Battery power

Not all electricity is produced in a power station. Some objects use batteries.

car battery

Batteries are different sizes for different things. The car battery is big.

Using a battery to make electricty means the object doesn't need a plug.

These torches use a battery so you can carry them about with you.

Electric circuits

An electric circuit shows how a battery can make a bulb light up.

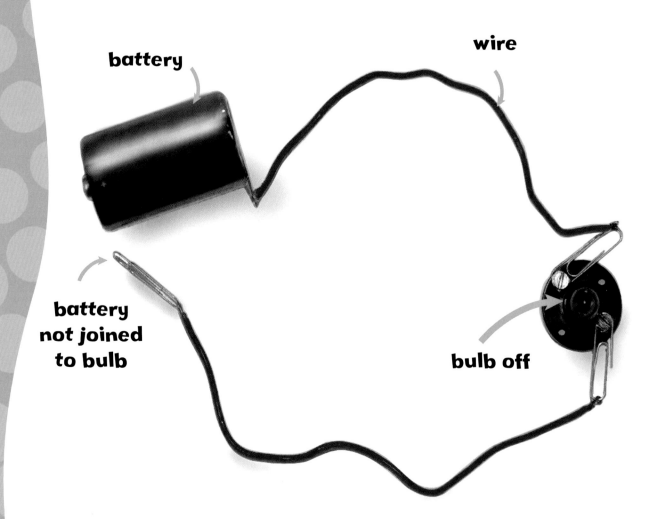

battery

wire

battery not joined to bulb

bulb off

▲ **A battery can light a bulb but only if wires join the battery and bulb together.**

Electricity flows through the wire from the battery to the bulb, so that the bulb lights up. Then the electricity flows back into the battery.

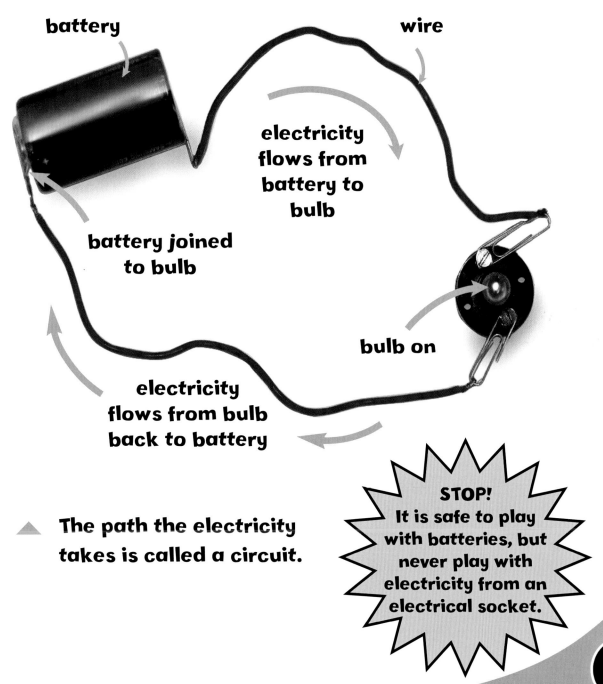

battery

wire

electricity flows from battery to bulb

battery joined to bulb

bulb on

electricity flows from bulb back to battery

▲ The path the electricity takes is called a circuit.

STOP!
It is safe to play with batteries, but never play with electricity from an electrical socket.

Switches

We use a switch to start or stop electricity flowing. A switch is like a bridge or gate in the circuit.

When the switch is down, the gap is closed and electricity flows round the circuit to work the motor.

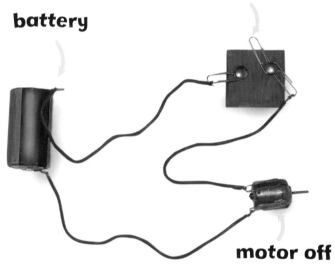

switch up

battery

motor off

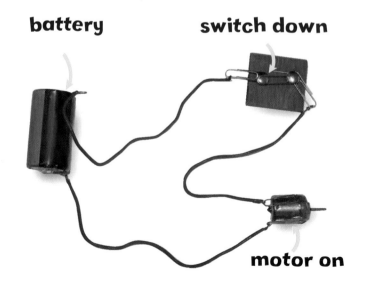

battery　　**switch down**

motor on

There are lots of switches in your home. When the switch is 'on', electricity flows and the light or machine starts to work.

Switches come in different shapes and sizes.

Plugs and sockets

Electricity comes from the pylons into our homes through sockets in the wall. To make the electricity flow, we have to put a plug in the socket and switch it on.

▶ **Some sockets have two holes in them, some have three holes.**

socket   **switch**

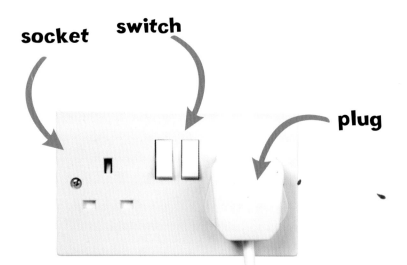

plug

▲ **Not all sockets have switches.**

Electricity makes tools, lights and machines work anywhere you can plug them in.

STOP!
Never push anything except a plug into an electric socket.

Electricity outdoors

Electricity works the lights of cars, buses and lorries. It also works streetlights, traffic lights and coloured signs.

▼ **Look at all the different electric lights below.**

Electricity makes this express train move.

▼ **This train has huge electric motors to make it go very fast.**

Things to do

Battery power

Which of these needs a battery to work?

a

b

c

d

It's electricity!

Put these pictures in the right order to show how we get electricity at home.

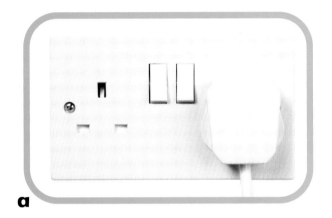

a

b

c

Talk back

How have you used electricity today?
Look around and name the objects that
need electricity to make them work.

Glossary

circuit A path that electricity flows along from a battery or socket so that a machine works when it is switched on.

hob Part of an electric cooker that can get very hot when it is switched on.

plug The part used to fit an electric wire into a socket.

socket Where an electric plug fits so that electricty can flow. Sometimes it has a switch.

Index